DEL REY
NEW YORK

Copyright © 2018 by Mojang AB and Mojang Synergies AB. MINECRAFT is a trademark or registered trademark of Mojang Synergies AB.

All rights reserved.

Published in the United States by Del Rey, an imprint of Random House, a division of Penguin Random House LLC, New York.

DEL REY and the HOUSE colophon are registered trademarks of Penguin Random House LLC.

Published in hardcover in the United Kingdom by Egmont UK Limited.

ISBN 978-1-101-96634-1
Ebook ISBN 978-1-101-96635-8

Printed in China on acid-free paper by C & C Offset

Written by Stephanie Milton. Additional material by Marsh Davies.

Illustrations by Ryan Marsh and Joe Bolder

randomhousebooks.com

4 6 8 9 7 5 3

Design by Joe Bolder

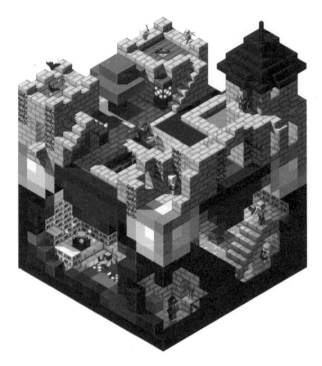

MOJANG
MINECRAFT

GUIDE TO:
ENCHANTMENTS & POTIONS

CONTENTS

INTRODUCTION

In theory, a bold adventurer can make their way through the world of Minecraft with little more than a pickaxe and a can-do attitude. In practice, though, such bold adventurers mostly end up as a pile of inventory items, bobbing in a dark pit surrounded by mobs – so it's probaly best to voyage into the unknown suitably equipped. That means learning how to affix your kit with arcane enchantments that let you deflect mighty blows, deal even more deadly damage, or even breathe underwater. A swig of a potion, meanwhile, can give you the power boost that means the difference between life and a lengthy trek back from your spawn point. Read on, and the mysteries of such magical arts will be revealed!

MARSH DAVIES
THE MOJANG TEAM

MOJANG STUFF

This super-exclusive info has come directly from the developers at Mojang.

1

ENCHANTMENTS

The mystical process of enchanting may seem daunting to beginners, but it's quite simple once you have the right equipment. Luckily, everything you need can be found in the Overworld. Let's take a look at the various methods of enchanting, the enchantments that are available for each item and when each enchantment will be most useful.

ENCHANTMENT MECHANICS

Enchantments are magical effects that improve the performance of your items, or provide them with extra abilities or uses. When used correctly they can really help to keep you alive in Survival mode. Enchanting is a fairly complicated process, so it's important to learn about the mechanics of the process before you begin.

MOJANG STUFF

As you play Minecraft you gain experience points, or XP. We should probably have called them enchantment points, however, as using them to power up your kit is really the only way you can spend them.

ENCHANTMENT METHODS

There are three methods you can use to enchant your items:

 You can enchant items on an enchantment table, in exchange for experience levels and lapis lazuli. This only works for items with no existing enchantments. Three options are available each time you use an enchantment table.

 You can combine two of the same item, each with a different enchantment, on an anvil. This will produce one item with two enchantments and costs experience levels.

 You can combine an enchanted book with an unenchanted item on an anvil, imbuing the item with the enchantment from the book (or multiple enchantments if the book carries more than one). This also costs experience levels.

MOJANG STUFF

There's an element of randomization to enchanting. Don't like what the enchantment table has available? Building another table won't help – but you can enchant some garbage item on the cheap and try your luck again!

WHAT CAN YOU ENCHANT?

You'll recognize enchanted items by their otherworldly purple glow. Enchantments can be added to most armor items, tools and weapons, and even books. Some items can be enchanted on a table or an anvil, others can only be enchanted on an anvil.

KEY

Can be enchanted on an enchantment table

Can be enchanted on an anvil

HELMET

CHESTPLATE

BOW

LEGGINGS/PANTS

BOOTS

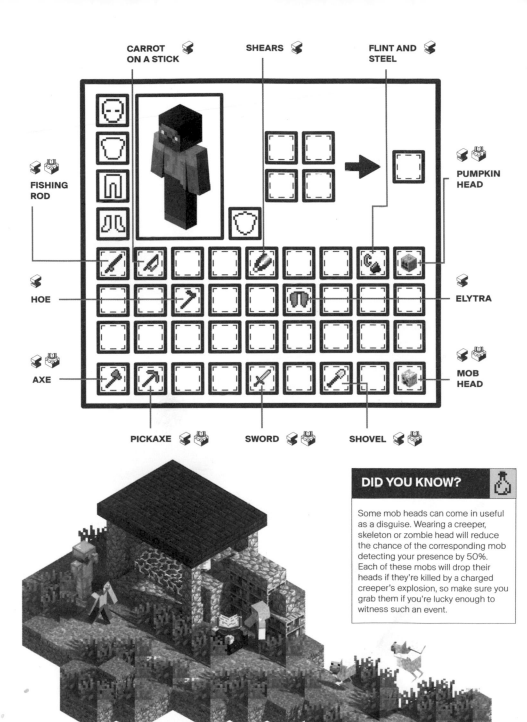

CARROT ON A STICK

SHEARS

FLINT AND STEEL

FISHING ROD

PUMPKIN HEAD

HOE

ELYTRA

AXE

MOB HEAD

PICKAXE

SWORD

SHOVEL

DID YOU KNOW?

Some mob heads can come in useful as a disguise. Wearing a creeper, skeleton or zombie head will reduce the chance of the corresponding mob detecting your presence by 50%. Each of these mobs will drop their heads if they're killed by a charged creeper's explosion, so make sure you grab them if you're lucky enough to witness such an event.

ENCHANTMENT POWER LEVEL

An enchantment's power level appears as a roman numeral next to its name. Some enchantments only have one power level (I), some three (III), others as many as five (V). The maximum power level for each enchantment is listed on pages 24-35.

The higher the power level, the more powerful the enchantment.

DIAMOND SWORD

FIRE ASPECT II
SMITE V

The power level will be visible in the enchantment's name – for example, Fire Aspect II is a power level 2 enchantment, and Smite V is a power level 5 enchantment.

ENCHANTMENT COST

Unfortunately, enchantments don't come for free – each has a different cost attached to it.

You pay for enchantments using your experience levels, which are an accumulation of the experience points you earn through mining, defeating mobs and other players, breeding, fishing and using furnaces.

You must be a certain experience level in order to access the enchantment in the first place. If an enchantment has a high level requirement it's a good indication that it will be a powerful enchantment, and that you will get multiple enchantments. It is not a guarantee, however, as there's also a random factor to the process.

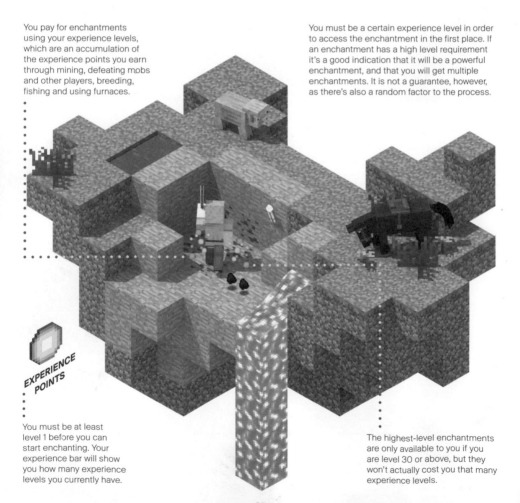

EXPERIENCE POINTS

You must be at least level 1 before you can start enchanting. Your experience bar will show you how many experience levels you currently have.

The highest-level enchantments are only available to you if you are level 30 or above, but they won't actually cost you that many experience levels.

The more experience levels you have, the more likely it is that higher-level enchantments will be available, although this isn't the only factor. See pages 20-21 to learn about the effect of bookshelves on an enchantment table.

 2 13

In this example you'll need 13 experience levels to be able to access the enchantment, but it will only cost you 2 experience levels (and 2 pieces of lapis lazuli).

ENCHANTMENT WEIGHT

Each enchantment has a weight, which tells you how likely it is to appear as an option when you enchant your items. The higher the weight of an enchantment, the more chance there is of it appearing. You can check the weight of each enchantment on pages 24-35.

PRIMARY AND SECONDARY ITEMS

Primary items can be enchanted in Survival mode via an enchantment table. Secondary items can't be enchanted on an enchantment table but can receive enchantments from enchanted books via an anvil. See pages 22-23 for more info.

ENCHANTABILITY

Different items and materials have different levels of enchantability. The higher the enchantability of an item, the greater the chance it will receive higher-level enchantments and multiple enchantments. This table shows the relative enchantability of various materials and items.

MATERIAL	ARMOR ENCHANTABILITY	SWORD/TOOL ENCHANTABILITY
WOOD	N/A	15
LEATHER	15	N/A
STONE	N/A	5
IRON	9	14
CHAIN	12	N/A
DIAMOND	10	10
GOLD	25	22
BOOK	1	1

As you can see, gold has the highest enchantability and is the easiest material to enchant, but gold tools, weapons and armor are the least durable and wear out quickly. Diamond has a lower enchantability but is the most durable material and will last much longer than gold.

Chainmail armor can't be crafted, but armorer villagers may offer it as a trade.

TREASURE ENCHANTMENTS

Treasure enchantments are rare – they will never be available through an enchantment table, but you may find items carrying these enchantments on your travels, if you know where to look.

You might reel in an item with a treasure enchantment when fishing.

Villagers may offer you items with treasure enchantments as part of their trades.

Items in naturally generated chests may carry treasure enchantments.

MULTIPLE ENCHANTMENTS

There's a good chance you'll get more than one enchantment on an item when using an enchantment table, but you won't know exactly what additional enchantments you're getting until you perform the enchantment. The maximum number of enchantments that a single item can carry is five.

DIAMOND SWORD
FIRE ASPECT II
SMITE V
KNOCKBACK II
LOOTING III

CONFLICTING ENCHANTMENTS

Some enchantments conflict with other enchantments, which means they cannot both be applied to the same item. Bear in mind the following rules when enchanting to avoid disappointment.

 Every enchantment conflicts with itself, so you can't add two of the same enchantment to one item.

 All protection enchantments conflict with each other, so you can only choose one per item. The protection enchantments are Blast Protection, Feather Falling, Fire Protection, Projectile Protection and Protection.

 All damage enchantments conflict with each other, so you can only choose one. Damage enchantments are Sharpness, Smite and Bane of Arthropods.

4 Silk Touch and Fortune conflict with each other.

5 Depth Strider and Frost Walker conflict with each other.

6 Mending and Infinity conflict with each other.

PROTECTION ENCHANTMENTS FOR ARMOR

Each protection enchantment listed in the table below provides an enchantment protection factor, or EPF for short. When protection enchantments have been applied to several pieces of armor that are being worn simultaneously, these EPFs add up and will be capped when they reach a maximum of 20. At this level, the damage you take is reduced by the maximum amount, which is 80%.

This table shows the EPF for each level of each protection enchantment.

ENCHANTMENT	DAMAGE REDUCED FOR	EPF LEVEL I	EPF LEVEL II	EPF LEVEL III	EPF LEVEL IV
Protection	All	1	2	3	4
Fire Protection	Fire, lava and blaze fireballs	2	4	6	8
Blast Protection	Explosions	2	4	6	8
Projectile Protection	Arrows, ghast and blaze fireballs	2	4	6	8
Feather Falling	Fall damage	3	6	9	12

Want to save yourself some materials? You can achieve maximum protection against certain types of damage using just three pieces of armor. For example, you can wear two pieces of armor enchanted with Blast Protection IV (each offers an EPF of 8) and one enchanted with Protection IV (EPF 4), giving you a total of 20 EPF against explosions. See pages 24, 27, 28 and 32 for a full explanation of each protection enchantment.

THE ENCHANTMENT TABLE METHOD

The most popular method of enchanting an unenchanted item is using an enchantment table. This mysterious block is expensive to craft but worth the investment as it opens up a magical new world of opportunities.

1 Track down some obsidian. It generates naturally wherever flowing water hits a lava source and you'll need a diamond pickaxe to mine it. Be very careful when mining obsidian – there's often lava in the block underneath or to the side.

2 Find some diamond ore. It generates below level 16 so you'll need to mine down to the bottom of the world. You'll need 2 diamonds, and each block of diamond ore will drop 1 diamond when mined with an iron pickaxe.

PAPER RECIPE

3

3 Craft some paper from sugar canes, or track some down in a stronghold library chest.

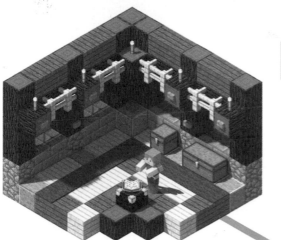

You'll need a good supply of lapis lazuli to pay for your enchantments, so make sure you stock up before you begin. Lapis lazuli ore generates at level 31 and below. When mined with a stone pickaxe or better, each block will drop 4-8 pieces of lapis lazuli.

LAPIS LAZULI

DID YOU KNOW?

Enchantment tables really do have mystical powers, and they can actually sense your presence. The book on top of the table will turn toward you and open when you approach.

6 Find a home for your enchantment table in your base. Position it in an area with a few blocks' space on each side so you can surround it with bookshelves later to access the highest-level enchantments (see pages 20-21 for more info).

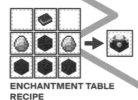

ENCHANTMENT TABLE RECIPE

5 Use your paper and leather to craft a book. Now you have everything you need to craft an enchantment table.

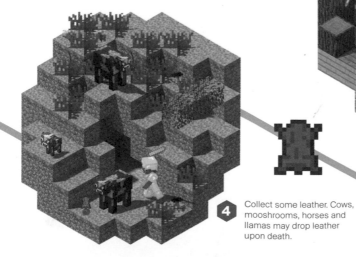

4 Collect some leather. Cows, mooshrooms, horses and llamas may drop leather upon death.

BOOK RECIPE

USING AN ENCHANTMENT TABLE

Now that your enchantment table is set up and you've mined all the lapis lazuli you can get your hands on, you're ready to start enchanting your items. Let's take a closer look at how this otherworldly block works.

When you interact with your enchantment table you'll be presented with an interface that looks like the one you can see below. Place the item you wish to enchant in the empty item slot, and three enchantment options will appear on the right for your consideration.

The enchantment options are written in the Standard Galactic Alphabet. Hover over them to see the name of one of the enchantments that will be applied if you choose that option. Although only one enchantment is visible, you may get more.

The required experience level (labeled as the "enchantment level" when you hover over the enchantment if you have enough experience levels, or "level requirement" if you don't) will be displayed to the right of each enchantment.

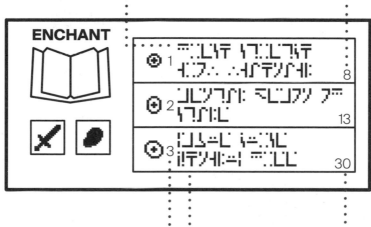

The number on the left of each enchantment tells you how many experience levels and pieces of lapis lazuli it costs.

You can only choose enchantments that are the same experience level or lower than your current experience level. Don't forget to check your experience bar to see which level you're currently at.

The lowest-level enchantment (always in the top slot) will cost 1 experience level and 1 lapis lazuli, the middle enchantment will cost 2 of each and the highest-level enchantment (always in the bottom slot) will cost 3.

Select one of the enchantment options that are available to you. You'll hear a strange noise and the lapis lazuli will disappear, along with the enchantment options. Drag your newly enchanted item back into your inventory.

THE STANDARD GALACTIC ALPHABET

The Standard Galactic Alphabet is a series of cryptic runes that was first used in the Commander Keen games. The runes used to describe each enchantment are a random combination of 3-5 words. They aren't actually relevant to the enchantment chosen and are there for decoration.

BOOKSHELVES

Enchantment tables have the curious ability to draw power from nearby bookshelves and use it to access higher-level enchantments. Exactly how this works is a bit of a mystery. With no bookshelves, the experience level requirement for an enchantment will never be more than 8, but with bookshelves it can be as high as 30.

BOOKSHELF RECIPE

See page 17 for a reminder of how to craft books, then craft books together with wood planks to make bookshelves. To access the highest-level enchantments you'll need 15 bookshelves, arranged in the proper position. Try the bookshelf square or the bookshelf corner shown here.

THE BOOKSHELF SQUARE

In this layout, the square of 15 bookshelves is 1 block high.

 There must be a block of air between each bookshelf and the enchantment table - even carpet will be enough to disable the effect of the bookshelves.

 You'll find bookshelves in some NPC village libraries, stronghold libraries and woodland mansions. When mined with an axe they'll drop their books, which can be crafted with wood planks to build new bookshelves.

THE BOOKSHELF CORNER

In this layout, 2 bookshelves are stacked on top of each other in each position, so the total number is 16. This is one more than is actually necessary to access the highest-level enchantments.

3 Each bookshelf increases the highest possible level requirement by 1-2 levels, up to a maximum of 30 levels with the full 15 bookshelves.

4 You'll know you've placed the bookshelves in the correct position when you see runes flow from the bookshelves into the table, imbuing it with power.

5 The bookshelves must either be on the same level or one block higher than the enchantment table.

THE ANVIL METHOD

There are two ways you can use an anvil to enchant items. You can combine an enchanted book with an unenchanted item, or you can combine two of the same item, each with different enchantments, to create one item that carries both.

Crafting an anvil will set you back 3 solid blocks of iron and an additional 4 iron ingots.

ANVIL

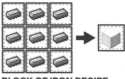

BLOCK OF IRON RECIPE

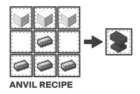

ANVIL RECIPE

1. COMBINING AN ENCHANTED BOOK WITH AN ITEM

An enchanted book is useful if you want a specific enchantment. You may come across enchanted books on your travels. If you don't have any items to enchant right now, but have lots of experience points, you might also choose to enchant a book and save it to apply to another item later.

ENCHANTED BOOK

You can enchant a regular book on an enchantment table. As with other items you'll be given three options and you may get multiple enchantments.

Make sure the enchantment on the enchanted book will work for the item you wish to enchant. For example, if the book is enchanted with respiration, it will only work on a helmet. If there are multiple enchantments on the book, only the enchantments that work for that item will be applied. You can read about enchantments and the items they can be applied to in the next few pages.

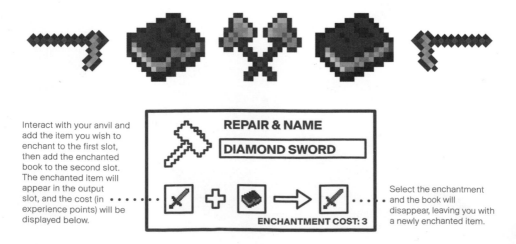

Interact with your anvil and add the item you wish to enchant to the first slot, then add the enchanted book to the second slot. The enchanted item will appear in the output slot, and the cost (in experience points) will be displayed below.

REPAIR & NAME

DIAMOND SWORD

ENCHANTMENT COST: 3

Select the enchantment and the book will disappear, leaving you with a newly enchanted item.

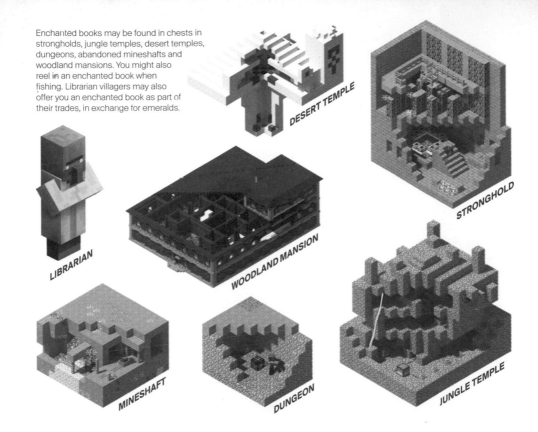

Enchanted books may be found in chests in strongholds, jungle temples, desert temples, dungeons, abandoned mineshafts and woodland mansions. You might also reel in an enchanted book when fishing. Librarian villagers may also offer you an enchanted book as part of their trades, in exchange for emeralds.

DESERT TEMPLE

STRONGHOLD

LIBRARIAN

WOODLAND MANSION

MINESHAFT

DUNGEON

JUNGLE TEMPLE

2. COMBINING TWO OF THE SAME ITEM WITH DIFFERENT ENCHANTMENTS

Once an item has been enchanted it can't be enchanted further using an enchantment table. That's where the anvil comes in handy yet again – it allows you to combine two of the same item with different enchantments. Add the items to the anvil slots and, if you have enough experience levels, the new item, carrying both enchantments, will appear in the output slot.

Slightly damaged anvil

Very damaged anvil

DID YOU KNOW?

Each time you use an anvil there's a chance that it will become damaged. Most anvils will last for 25 uses before being destroyed. Look for signs that your anvil is taking damage, and when it appears very damaged you'll know it's time to craft a new one.

REPAIRING ENCHANTED ITEMS

You can also repair enchanted items on an anvil, either by combining two of the same item (one will be sacrificed) or by using some of the material the item has been crafted from to repair it (e.g., iron ingots will repair an enchanted iron pickaxe). You can keep adding material such as iron ingots until the item is completely repaired, or just use one or two to slightly increase its remaining lifespan.

ENCHANTMENTS AND THEIR USES

So you have everything you need to start producing powerful enchanted tools, weapons and armor to give you a supernatural edge. Let's take a look at what each enchantment does and how it can help you.

AQUA AFFINITY

PRIMARY ITEMS	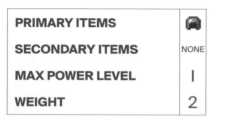
SECONDARY ITEMS	NONE
MAX POWER LEVEL	I
WEIGHT	2

Aqua Affinity increases the rate at which you can mine blocks when you're underwater. You'll be able to break blocks that are submerged in water at the same speed as if they were situated on land. This is particularly useful if you're mining large quantities of clay from river beds, or if you're mining in ocean monuments.

BANE OF ARTHROPODS

PRIMARY ITEMS	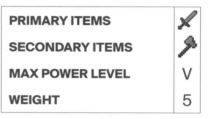
SECONDARY ITEMS	
MAX POWER LEVEL	V
WEIGHT	5

This enchantment increases the damage to arthropod mobs – that means spiders, cave spiders, silverfish and endermites. It also inflicts Slowness IV on the mob, which slows their movement. It lasts between 1 and 1.5 seconds at level I. The maximum duration will increase by half a second for each level, up to a maximum of 3.5 seconds at level V.

BLAST PROTECTION

PRIMARY ITEMS	
SECONDARY ITEMS	NONE
MAX POWER LEVEL	IV
WEIGHT	2

Blast Protection reduces the damage you'll take from explosions caused by TNT and creeper detonation. It also reduces the knockback caused by these explosions. It's a handy enchantment to use when you might come into contact with creepers or enemy players.

CURSE OF BINDING

PRIMARY ITEMS	NONE
SECONDARY ITEMS	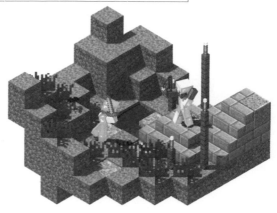
MAX POWER LEVEL	I
WEIGHT	1

When applied to an item, the Curse of Binding will prevent the item from being removed from a player once it's been equipped in an armor slot. The only way an item carrying this curse can be removed is if it's broken, or if the player wearing it dies and respawns. This may not sound terrible, but it comes in handy when you're fighting other players as it means you can trick your opponents into getting stuck wearing low durability leather armor or pumpkin heads during PVP (player versus player) battles.

CURSE OF VANISHING

PRIMARY ITEMS	NONE
SECONDARY ITEMS	
MAX POWER LEVEL	I
WEIGHT	1

The Curse of Vanishing enchantment causes the tool, weapon or piece of armor to be destroyed when the player dies. It's best used during PVP battles as it will prevent enemy players getting their hands on your best equipment. If you want to trade your Curse of Vanishing armor with a friend, you can drop it on the ground and they'll be able to pick it up in the usual way.

ITEMS	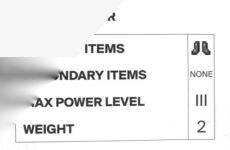
...NDARY ITEMS	NONE
...AX POWER LEVEL	III
WEIGHT	2

Depth Strider increases a player's movement speed when they're underwater. Each level of the enchantment reduces the amount the water slows you down by a third, and if you use level III you'll be able to swim as fast as you would usually walk on dry land. This is another great enchantment to try out if you're planning to visit an ocean monument as it means you'll be able to navigate as quickly as possible.

EFFICIENCY

PRIMARY ITEMS	
SECONDARY ITEMS	
MAX POWER LEVEL	V
WEIGHT	10

The Efficiency enchantment increases your mining speed when you're mining blocks that drop an item rather than themselves, e.g., coal ore and glowstone. You must use the most efficient tool when mining the block in question, e.g., a shovel for gravel or an axe for wood. This is the perfect enchantment to use when you're out collecting large quantities of resources for crafting as it will save you valuable time.

FEATHER FALLING

PRIMARY ITEMS	🥾🥾
SECONDARY ITEMS	NONE
MAX POWER LEVEL	IV
WEIGHT	5

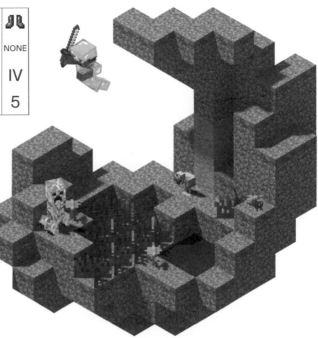

When applied to boots, the Feather Falling enchantment reduces the damage you take when you fall from a height, e.g., from a ledge when mining or off a cliff. It also reduces any damage you might take from teleporting using an ender pearl. It's a great all-purpose enchantment to use on your boots when exploring the world in Survival mode.

FIRE ASPECT

PRIMARY ITEMS	🗡️
SECONDARY ITEMS	NONE
MAX POWER LEVEL	II
WEIGHT	2

When you strike an enemy player or mob with a Fire Aspect sword, they will promptly be set on fire. Each level of the enchantment adds 80 fireticks – that's 4 seconds of burning time. Power level I will cause 3 points of damage, and power level II will cause 7. It's great for use in any dangerous situation, but if you kill an animal using a Fire Aspect sword it will drop cooked meat. Nether mobs are immune to burning so they won't take damage from this enchantment.

FIRE PROTECTION

PRIMARY ITEMS	
SECONDARY ITEMS	NONE
MAX POWER LEVEL	IV
WEIGHT	2

As its name suggests, the Fire Protection enchantment reduces the damage you take from lava or sources of fire. It also reduces the amount of time that you'll be on fire. Fire Protection is recommended for a trip to the Nether, and when mining at the bottom of the Overworld, where lava is abundant.

FLAME

PRIMARY ITEMS	
SECONDARY ITEMS	NONE
MAX POWER LEVEL	I
WEIGHT	2

Arrows fired from a bow enchanted with Flame will be flaming arrows. Each arrow deals 4 fire damage points to its target over the course of 5 seconds. Flaming arrows will only have an effect on mobs, players and TNT blocks and won't set wood or any other blocks ablaze. This enchantment is ideal for use on a bow for PVP battles or mob battles in the Overworld. Remember that Nether mobs are immune to burning so won't take any damage from a flame bow.

FORTUNE

PRIMARY ITEMS	⛏ 🪓 🔨
SECONDARY ITEMS	NONE
MAX POWER LEVEL	III
WEIGHT	2

The Fortune enchantment will increase the chance of getting more drops from a block you're mining – this includes ores and crops. It will also increase the chance that leaf blocks will drop saplings and oak leaves will drop apples, so it's a great enchantment to use when you're out collecting resources.

FROST WALKER

PRIMARY ITEMS	NONE
SECONDARY ITEMS	👢
MAX POWER LEVEL	II
WEIGHT	2

The Frost Walker enchantment creates frosted ice blocks beneath your feet when you walk or run across water blocks, so it's very useful when you need to travel across large areas of water. It also prevents you taking damage from magma blocks in the Nether.

INFINITY

PRIMARY ITEMS	🏹
SECONDARY ITEMS	NONE
MAX POWER LEVEL	I
WEIGHT	1

Infinity allows you to fire an infinite number of regular arrows from your bow, as long as you have 1 regular arrow in your inventory. Try it out when dealing with skeletons or during PVP combat. Unfortunately it doesn't work on tipped or spectral arrows.

KNOCKBACK

PRIMARY ITEMS	🗡
SECONDARY ITEMS	NONE
MAX POWER LEVEL	II
WEIGHT	5

This enchantment increases the knockback of your sword (the amount a player or mob is pushed backward, away from you, when hit). The effect of Knockback should not be underestimated – it's possible to knock players or mobs over cliffs or into lava. This is a great enchantment for any combat situation.

LOOTING

PRIMARY ITEMS	⚔️
SECONDARY ITEMS	NONE
MAX POWER LEVEL	III
WEIGHT	2

Looting causes an increase in mob drops. It increases the maximum number of common drops by 1 per power level and increases the chance of uncommon drops by causing a second attempt if the first fails. It also increases the chance of getting rare drops and equipment drops. It's best used when you need specific mob drops that are difficult to get, e.g., potion ingredients.

LUCK OF THE SEA

PRIMARY ITEMS	🎣
SECONDARY ITEMS	NONE
MAX POWER LEVEL	III
WEIGHT	2

The Luck of the Sea enchantment increases your luck when fishing. This means your chance of reeling in junk items and fish is lower than usual, whereas your chance of reeling in treasure items is higher. Treasure items include bows, enchanted books, fishing rods, name tags, saddles and lily pads, so this enchantment can provide you with some really useful items.

LURE

PRIMARY ITEMS	🎣
SECONDARY ITEMS	NONE
MAX POWER LEVEL	III
WEIGHT	2

The Lure enchantment increases the number of fish that will bite at your fishing rod. It also decreases the time you have to wait for a catch by 5 seconds per power level. Take this one with you on a fishing expedition and you'll soon have all the fish you could possibly need.

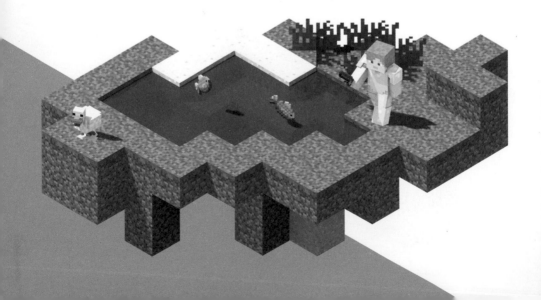

MENDING

PRIMARY ITEMS	NONE
SECONDARY ITEMS	
MAX POWER LEVEL	I
WEIGHT	2

When an item that's enchanted with Mending is held or worn it will be repaired using the experience points you earn. The rate of repair is 2 durability points per experience point. You won't accrue experience points while you're using this enchantment, but once the Mending item is fully repaired your experience points will begin to accrue again. This is a great enchantment to use when you're short on resources to craft more items.

POWER

PRIMARY ITEMS	
SECONDARY ITEMS	NONE
MAX POWER LEVEL	V
WEIGHT	10

The Power enchantment increases arrow damage by 25% x (power level +1), rounded up to the nearest half heart. So, if your bow is Power level I, the damage is increased by 50% (25 x 2). For level II it's 75% (25 x 3), and so on. It's a great enchantment to use when fighting off hostile mobs or enemy players. You'll need an anvil if you want to apply level V.

PROJECTILE PROTECTION

PRIMARY ITEMS	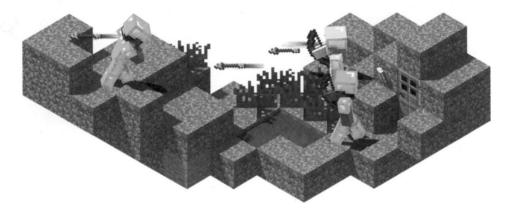
SECONDARY ITEMS	NONE
MAX POWER LEVEL	IV
WEIGHT	5

Projectile Protection reduces the damage you sustain from projectiles (arrows, ghast or blaze fireballs, fire charges). It's a great enchantment to use in PVP battles if your opponents have bows, when fighting skeletons, or in the Nether.

PROTECTION

PRIMARY ITEMS	
SECONDARY ITEMS	NONE
MAX POWER LEVEL	IV
WEIGHT	10

The Protection enchantment reduces all damage, except for hunger damage and damage sustained by falling into the Void. This is an all-purpose enchantment that is a valuable addition to your armor for any dangerous situation.

PUNCH

PRIMARY ITEMS	
SECONDARY ITEMS	NONE
MAX POWER LEVEL	II
WEIGHT	2

The Punch enchantment increases the knockback effect of your bow and arrow, so mobs and players are knocked back further than they would usually be. It's a great enchantment for any combat situation where you're keen to keep your opponents as far away from you as possible.

RESPIRATION

PRIMARY ITEMS	
SECONDARY ITEMS	NONE
MAX POWER LEVEL	III
WEIGHT	2

Respiration extends the amount of time you are able to survive underwater without breathing, by providing you with an additional 15 seconds per power level. It also improves your visibility. It's extremely useful if you plan to venture underwater, e.g., to visit an ocean monument.

SHARPNESS

PRIMARY ITEMS	
SECONDARY ITEMS	
MAX POWER LEVEL	V
WEIGHT	10

The Sharpness enchantment increases the damage dealt by your sword or axe, making it a more effective weapon for combat situations. It adds 1 extra point of damage for the first power level, and half a point for each additional power level. You'll need an anvil to apply power level V.

SILK TOUCH

PRIMARY ITEMS	
SECONDARY ITEMS	
MAX POWER LEVEL	III
WEIGHT	1

Silk Touch causes many blocks that would usually drop items to drop themselves instead. It can be used on coal ore, diamond ore, emerald ore, grass, huge mushrooms, ice, lapis lazuli ore, mycelium, packed ice, podzol, Nether quartz ore, redstone ore and cobwebs. Ender chests, bookshelves, glass and glass panes can only be retrieved by using Silk Touch once placed.

SMITE

PRIMARY ITEMS	⚔
SECONDARY ITEMS	🔨
MAX POWER LEVEL	V
WEIGHT	5

SWEEPING EDGE

PRIMARY ITEMS	⚔
SECONDARY ITEMS	NONE
MAX POWER LEVEL	III
WEIGHT	1

Smite increases the damage your sword or axe does to undead mobs (skeletons, zombies, withers, wither skeletons and zombie pigmen). It's particularly handy for trips to the Nether. You'll need an anvil for Smite V.

Sweeping Edge increases the sweeping attack damage of your sword. It's highly effective when battling hostile mobs or in PVP combat as it decreases the time it takes you to defeat your opponents.

THORNS

PRIMARY ITEMS	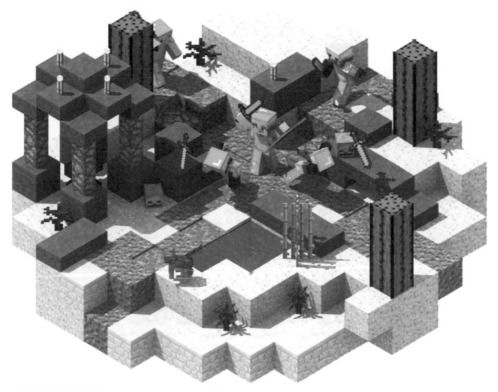
SECONDARY ITEMS	
MAX POWER LEVEL	III
WEIGHT	1

Thorns inflicts damage on any player or mob that attacks you by melee (hand to hand) attack or projectile. It will reduce your armor's durability. You'll need an anvil to create Thorns III by combining two Thorns II enchantments, or trading for an enchanted book from a villager.

UNBREAKING

PRIMARY ITEMS	
SECONDARY ITEMS	
MAX POWER LEVEL	III
WEIGHT	5

Unbreaking increases the effective durability of your armor, tool or weapon. It's a great all-purpose enchantment that can be used when gathering resources or in combat situations.

NATURALLY OCCURRING ENCHANTED ITEMS

If you find yourself without the necessary equipment or experience levels to enchant your items, don't despair. There are plenty of naturally generated enchanted items just waiting to be discovered. Let's get hunting!

VILLAGER TRADING

Some villagers will offer enchanted items as part of their trades. Fishermen may offer enchanted fishing rods, librarians enchanted books, armorers pieces of enchanted armor, etc. Villages can be found in desert, plains, savanna, taiga and ice plains biomes.

FISHING

There's even treasure hidden in the water – you might catch an enchanted book, bow or fishing rod when fishing.

DID YOU KNOW?

Clerics may offer you a curious item called a bottle o'enchanting as a fourth-tier trade. When thrown at any non-liquid block, it will drop experience orbs worth 3-11 experience points. They'll set you back 3-11 emeralds, but they're really handy if you're low on experience points and need to enchant some items.

MOB DROPS

Zombies, skeletons and zombie pigmen may drop items of enchanted armor or weapons when they die.

END CITY CHESTS

When visiting End cities on the outer islands you may find enchanted items of armor or enchanted tools or weapons in the loot chests.

POTIONS

Potions aren't just for witches – with your newfound knowledge of enchanting, you're ready to brave the Nether and collect materials you need to brew your very own supply of potions. These drinkable items will give you even more of an edge in Survival mode.

BREWING EQUIPMENT

Brewing is the magical process of creating potions – drinkable items that provide you with temporary status effects. It's a complicated business, so before we get into the details of the process, let's take a look at the equipment you'll need.

 Potions are made on a brewing stand, which is crafted from a blaze rod and cobblestone. Blaze rods are dropped by blazes in the Nether when they die. Blazes spawn from spawners in Nether fortresses.

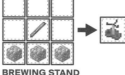

BREWING STAND RECIPE

2 You'll need a cauldron, which you can craft from iron ingots. You might also find a cauldron in a witch hut, an igloo basement or a woodland mansion.

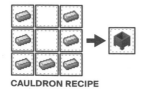

CAULDRON RECIPE

TIP

Your cauldron will need to be refilled frequently so make sure you have a water source like a pond or lake nearby.

3 You'll need a water bucket to fill your cauldron.

BUCKET RECIPE

4 Use glass bottles on a cauldron to create water bottles – the first step to creating every potion.

3

GLASS BOTTLE RECIPE

5 To power the brewing stand you'll need blaze powder. Each piece of blaze powder will last for 20 operations. Blaze powder can be crafted from a blaze rod.

2

BLAZE POWDER RECIPE

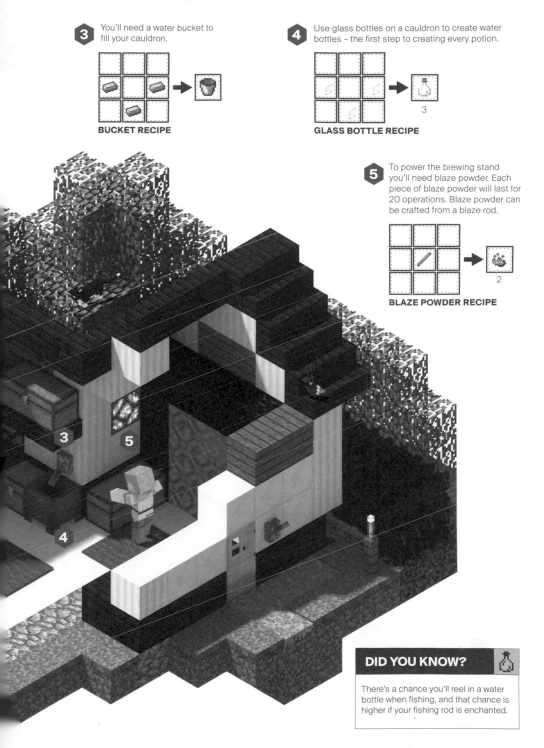

DID YOU KNOW?

There's a chance you'll reel in a water bottle when fishing, and that chance is higher if your fishing rod is enchanted.

INGREDIENTS

Before you can make usable potions you'll need to brew base potions by adding a single base ingredient to a water bottle. There are four base ingredients and four base potions. Mysteriously, only two of the base potions currently have a use . . .

BASE INGREDIENTS AND BASE POTIONS

NETHER WART

Nether wart is the base ingredient necessary to create most potions. It grows on soul sand under staircases in Nether fortresses and can also be found in loot chests in Nether fortresses.

AWKWARD POTION

When added to 3 water bottles, Nether wart makes 3 awkward potions. Awkward potion is the base for all potions except for potion of weakness.

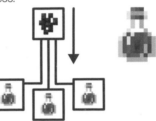

> **TIP**
>
> Grab a few blocks of soul sand from the Nether and take them back to the Overworld, then you can set up your own Nether wart.

GLOWSTONE DUST

Mine glowstone blocks in the Nether to get glowstone dust.

THICK POTION

When added to 3 water bottles, glowstone dust creates 3 thick potions. This potion currently has no use.

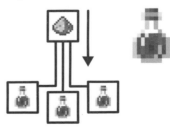

REDSTONE

Redstone can be obtained by mining redstone ore blocks, which can be found at level 16 and below.

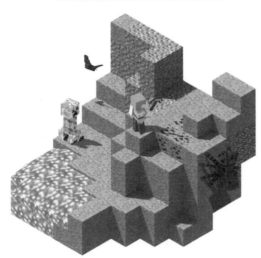

MUNDANE POTION

When added to 3 water bottles, redstone produces 3 mundane potions, which currently have no use. Mundane potion can also be brewed from 3 water bottles and any secondary ingredient. See pages 44-45 for a full list.

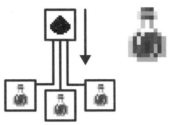

FERMENTED SPIDER EYE

A fermented spider eye can be crafted from a spider eye, sugar and a brown mushroom. Spiders may drop their eyes when killed.

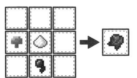

FERMENTED SPIDER EYE RECIPE

POTION OF WEAKNESS

Add a fermented spider eye to 3 water bottles to produce 3 potions of weakness. This potion reduces all melee attacks by 4 damage points and lasts for 1 minute 30 seconds.

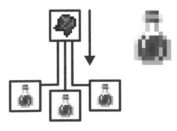

TIP

Potions don't stack in your inventory so make sure you clear some space before you start brewing.

SECONDARY INGREDIENTS AND MODIFIERS

Awkwardly, an awkward potion has no effect on its own; you'll need to brew it with a secondary ingredient to create a usable secondary potion. Secondary potions can then be brewed with a modifying ingredient to strengthen or change their effects. You'll need a good supply of all the ingredients you can see on this page.

SECONDARY INGREDIENTS

Sugar can be crafted from sugar canes. Witches sometimes drop sugar upon death.

Pufferfish can be caught when fishing. Guardians and elder guardians will sometimes drop pufferfish when they die.

A rabbit's foot is a rare item that may be dropped by rabbits when they die.

SUGAR RECIPE

GOLD NUGGET RECIPE

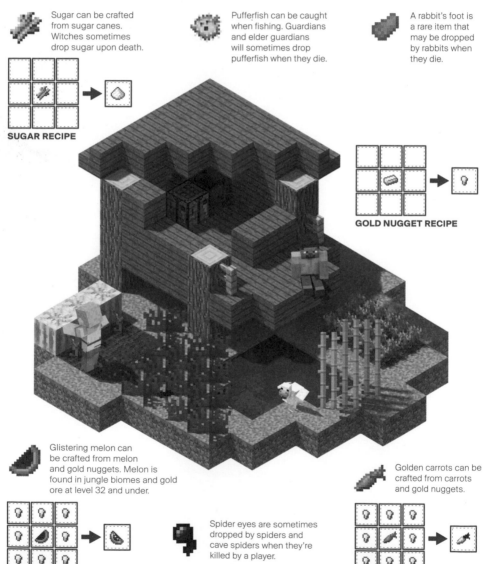

Glistering melon can be crafted from melon and gold nuggets. Melon is found in jungle biomes and gold ore at level 32 and under.

Spider eyes are sometimes dropped by spiders and cave spiders when they're killed by a player.

Golden carrots can be crafted from carrots and gold nuggets.

GLISTERING MELON RECIPE

GOLDEN CARROT RECIPE

44

Magma cream is sometimes dropped by big and small magma cubes in the Nether.

Ghast tears are occasionally dropped by ghasts upon death.

Blaze powder can be crafted from blaze rods, which may be dropped by blazes when they die.

MODIFIERS

Brewing a secondary potion with redstone will make its effects last longer.

Glowstone dust increases a potion's potency, so its effects are stronger.

Dragon's breath turns a regular potion into a lingering potion. See pages 60-61 for more info.

Fermented spider eye corrupts the effect of a potion – this usually means the effect is reversed to create a harmful potion. See page 43 for a reminder of the recipe.

Brewing a secondary potion with gunpowder will turn it into a splash potion. See pages 58-59 for more info about splash potions. Gunpowder is sometimes dropped by creepers and ghasts when they die.

SECONDARY POTIONS

Now the real fun can begin – you're ready to start brewing secondary potions. These potions can have either helpful or harmful effects and can get you out of all sorts of tricky situations. Here's a rundown of each potion and its effects.

HELPFUL SECONDARY POTIONS

FIRE RESISTANCE

INGREDIENTS	Awkward potion & magma cream
STATUS EFFECT	Fire resistance
DURATION	3 minutes

Potion of fire resistance provides you with immunity against fire damage, lava damage and ranged blaze attacks. It's extremely useful for trips to the Nether.

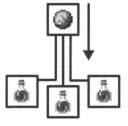

HEALING

INGREDIENTS	Awkward potion & glistering melon
STATUS EFFECT	Instant health
DURATION	Instant

A potion of healing will immediately restore 4 health points. This is a useful potion to keep in your inventory at all times in Survival mode.

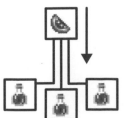

LEAPING

INGREDIENTS	Awkward potion & rabbit's foot
STATUS EFFECT	Jump boost
DURATION	3 minutes

Drink this potion and you'll be able to jump half a block higher than usual. This means you can clear obstacles like fences in a single leap.

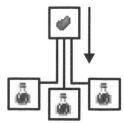

👁 NIGHT VISION

INGREDIENTS	Awkward potion & golden carrot
STATUS EFFECT	Night vision
DURATION	3 minutes

Drink this potion and everything will appear at maximum light level, including underwater areas. It's great for use at night, when mining and when swimming underwater.

 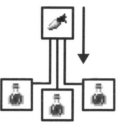

🖤 REGENERATION

INGREDIENTS	Awkward potion & ghast tear
STATUS EFFECT	Regeneration
DURATION	45 seconds

Regeneration restores your health over time (by around 2 health points every 2.4 seconds). It's particularly useful in situations where you might lose health points quite quickly.

 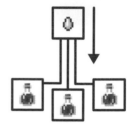

🗡 STRENGTH

INGREDIENTS	Awkward potion & blaze powder
STATUS EFFECT	Strength
DURATION	3 minutes

Potion of strength increases the damage you deal to your opponents through melee attacks by 3 health points. Drink this before battling other players or mobs.

 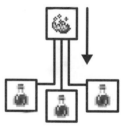

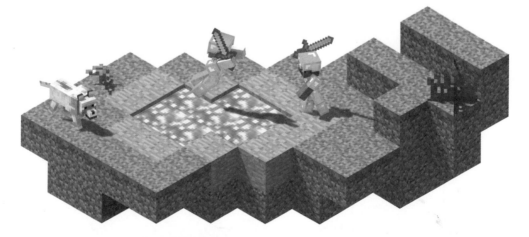

 **SWIFTNESS**

INGREDIENTS	Awkward potion & sugar
STATUS EFFECT	Speed
DURATION	3 minutes

Potion of swiftness increases your movement speed, sprinting speed and jumping length by around 20%. This is a good potion to drink if you're setting off on a long journey.

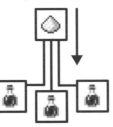

WATER BREATHING

INGREDIENTS	Awkward potion & pufferfish
STATUS EFFECT	Water breathing
DURATION	3 minutes

Drink this potion to top up your oxygen bar for 3 minutes. This makes exploring underwater areas such as ocean monuments significantly easier.

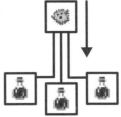

HARMFUL SECONDARY POTIONS

Unsurprisingly, harmful potions aren't going to do you any favors, so you're not going to want to drink them. Instead, they're best used as weapons against your opponents in the form of splash potions or lingering potions – see pages 58-61 to find out more.

♥ POISON

INGREDIENTS	Awkward potion & spider eye
STATUS EFFECT	Poison
DURATION	45 seconds

This potion will poison a player, reducing their health by around 1 point every 1.5 seconds, to 1 point at most.

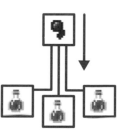

WEAKNESS (EXTENDED)

INGREDIENTS	Potion of weakness & redstone
STATUS EFFECT	Weakness
DURATION	4 minutes

The extended potion of weakness reduces all melee attacks by 4 damage points and lasts for 4 minutes.

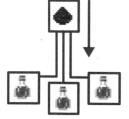

TERTIARY POTIONS

Tertiary potions are stronger versions of secondary potions – their effects last longer or they're more powerful. Favored by pro Minecrafters, they're made by brewing a modifying ingredient either with a secondary potion or with another tertiary potion.

HELPFUL TERTIARY POTIONS

⚫ FIRE RESISTANCE (EXTENDED)

INGREDIENTS	Potion of fire resistance & redstone
STATUS EFFECT	Fire resistance
DURATION	8 minutes

This potion gives the drinker immunity to damage from fire, lava and ranged blaze attacks for 8 minutes. It's a popular choice for adventurers visiting the Nether.

❤️ HEALING II

INGREDIENTS	Potion of healing & glowstone dust
STATUS EFFECT	Instant health II
DURATION	Instant

This restores 8 health points per potion (double the amount of regular potion of healing). It's great for any situation in which you're taking damage.

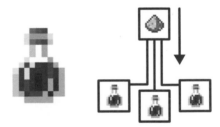

⚙️ INVISIBILITY

INGREDIENTS	Potion of night vision & fermented spider eye
STATUS EFFECT	Invisibility
DURATION	3 minutes

Technically, this is the corrupted version of potion of night vision. The drinker will be invisible to mobs and other players, but any equipped or held items will still be visible.

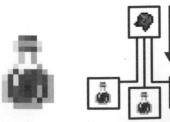

 INVISIBILITY (EXTENDED)

INGREDIENTS	Potion of night vision (extended) & fermented spider eye
ALTERNATIVE RECIPE	Potion of night vision & redstone
STATUS EFFECT	Invisibility
DURATION	8 minutes

The extended potion of invisibility will render the drinker invisible for 5 minutes longer than the regular version.

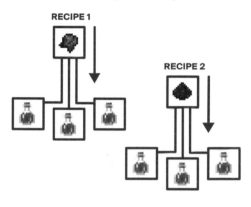

LEAPING (EXTENDED)

INGREDIENTS	Potion of leaping or potion of leaping II & redstone
STATUS EFFECT	Jump boost
DURATION	8 minutes

Drink this potion and you'll be able to jump half a block higher than usual. This means you can clear obstacles like fences in a single leap.

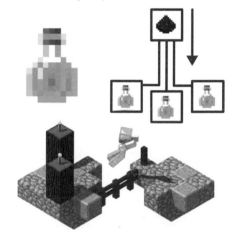

LEAPING II

INGREDIENTS	Potion of leaping & glowstone dust
STATUS EFFECT	Jump boost II
DURATION	1 minute 30 seconds

This potion enables the drinker to jump 1.5 blocks higher than usual. Note that the duration has decreased but the strength has increased.

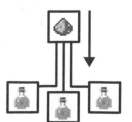

NIGHT VISION (EXTENDED)

INGREDIENTS	Potion of night vision & redstone
STATUS EFFECT	Night vision
DURATION	8 minutes

The extended potion of night vision lasts 5 minutes longer than the regular version. It makes everything appear to be at the maximum light level, including underwater areas.

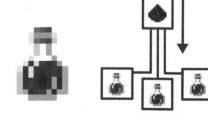

REGENERATION (EXTENDED)

INGREDIENTS	Potion of regeneration & redstone
STATUS EFFECT	Regeneration
DURATION	2 minutes

This restores the drinker's health over time by approximately 2 health points every 2.4 seconds. It lasts twice as long as the regular version.

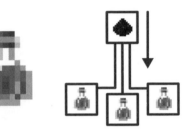

REGENERATION II

INGREDIENTS	Potion of regeneration & glowstone dust
STATUS EFFECT	Regeneration II
DURATION	22 seconds

The drinker's health is restored over time by around 2 health points every 1.2 seconds (that's more frequently than regular potion of regeneration).

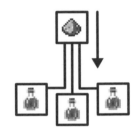

STRENGTH (EXTENDED)

INGREDIENTS	Potion of strength & redstone
STATUS EFFECT	Strength
DURATION	8 minutes

The extended potion of strength increases the damage you deal through melee attacks by 3 health points, and lasts 5 minutes longer than the regular version.

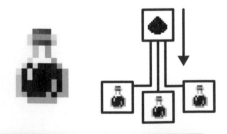

STRENGTH II

INGREDIENTS	Potion of strength & glowstone dust
STATUS EFFECT	Strength II
DURATION	1 minute 30 seconds

Strength II increases the damage you deal through melee attacks by 6 health points – that's double the amount of a regular potion of strength but doesn't last as long.

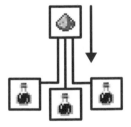

MOJANG STUFF

Originally the ingredients needed in brewing were going to be randomized every time you started a new world, so the result would always be a surprise when you combined ingredients. But this just wasn't as fun as we'd hoped it would be!

SWIFTNESS (EXTENDED)

INGREDIENTS	Potion of swiftness & redstone
STATUS EFFECT	Speed
DURATION	8 minutes

This increases a player's movement, sprinting speed and jumping length by approximately 20%, allowing for quicker travel across long distances.

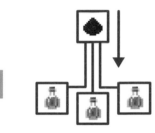

SWIFTNESS II

INGREDIENTS	Potion of swiftness & glowstone dust
STATUS EFFECT	Speed II
DURATION	1 minute 30 seconds

The drinker's movement, sprinting speed and jumping length will increase by around 40%, but it only lasts for a fraction of the time that the extended version lasts.

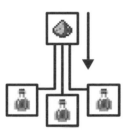

WATER BREATHING (EXTENDED)

INGREDIENTS	Potion of water breathing & redstone
STATUS EFFECT	Water breathing
DURATION	8 minutes

This potion ensures the player's oxygen bar doesn't deplete when they're underwater. It lasts 5 minutes longer than regular potion of water breathing.

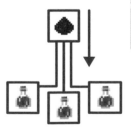

HARMFUL TERTIARY POTIONS

♥ HARMING

INGREDIENTS	Potion of healing & fermented spider eye
ALTERNATIVE RECIPE	Potion of poison (base or extended) & fermented spider eye
STATUS EFFECT	Instant damage
DURATION	Instant

Technically, potion of harming is the reverted form of potion of healing or potion of poison. This potion inflicts 6 points of damage.

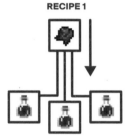

Technically, potion of harming is the reverted form of potion of healing or potion of poison. This potion inflicts 6 points of damage.

RECIPE 1 RECIPE 2

♥ HARMING II

INGREDIENTS	Potion of healing II & fermented spider eye
ALTERNATIVE RECIPE	Potion of poison II & fermented spider eye
ALTERNATIVE RECIPE 2	Potion of harming & glowstone dust
STATUS EFFECT	Instant damage II
DURATION	Instant

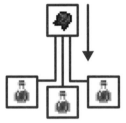

This potion inflicts 12 points of damage on the recipient – that's double the amount of a regular potion of harming.

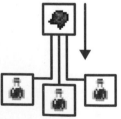

RECIPE 1

RECIPE 2

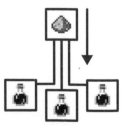

RECIPE 3

INGREDIENTS	Potion of poison & redstone
STATUS EFFECT	Poison
DURATION	2 minutes

INGREDIENTS	Potion of poison & glowstone dust
STATUS EFFECT	Poison
DURATION	22 seconds

This potion poisons the player, reducing their health to a minimum of 1 point, at a rate of approximately 1 point every 1.5 seconds.

This potion poisons the player, reducing their health to a minimum of 1 point, at a rate of approximately 2 health points every 1.5 seconds.

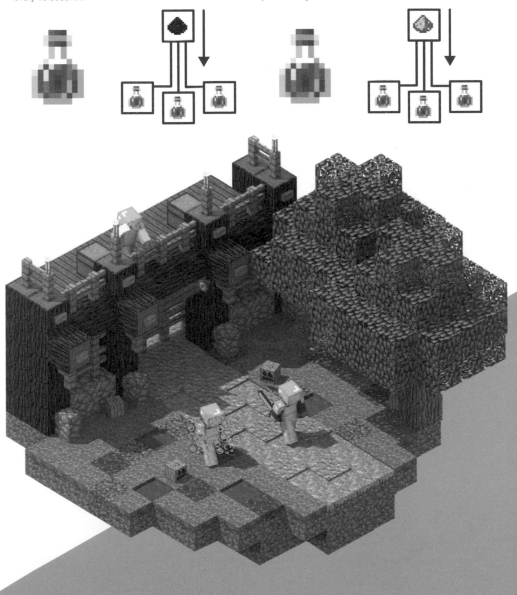

SLOWNESS

INGREDIENTS	Potion of swiftness & fermented spider eye
ALTERNATIVE RECIPE	Potion of leaping & fermented spider eye
STATUS EFFECT	Slowness
DURATION	1 minute 30 seconds

Slowness reduces the player's movement to a crouch (-15% speed).

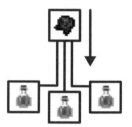

RECIPE 1

RECIPE 2

SLOWNESS (EXTENDED)

INGREDIENTS	Potion of slowness & redstone
ALTERNATIVE RECIPE	Potion of swiftness (extended) & fermented spider eye
ALTERNATIVE RECIPE 2	Potion of leaping (extended) & fermented spider eye
STATUS EFFECT	Slowness
DURATION	4 minutes

This slows the player's movement to a crouch (-15% speed) for twice as long as the regular potion of slowness.

RECIPE 1

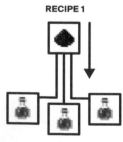

RECIPE 2

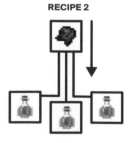

RECIPE 3

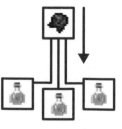

EFFICIENT BREWING

As we've seen, there's often more than one way to brew a potion. This chart shows the most efficient way to create each potion.

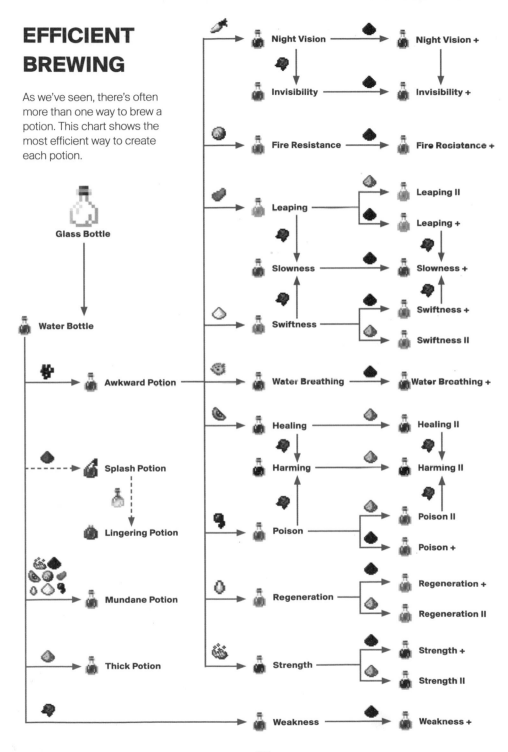

Glass Bottle

Water Bottle

Awkward Potion

Splash Potion

Lingering Potion

Mundane Potion

Thick Potion

Weakness

Night Vision → Night Vision +

Invisibility → Invisibility +

Fire Resistance → Fire Resistance +

Leaping → Leaping II

Leaping +

Slowness → Slowness +

Swiftness → Swiftness +

Swiftness II

Water Breathing → Water Breathing +

Healing → Healing II

Harming → Harming II

Poison → Poison II

Poison +

Regeneration → Regeneration +

Regeneration II

Strength → Strength +

Strength II

Weakness +

SPLASH POTIONS

Wouldn't it be great if you could trick your opponents into drinking harmful potions to bring about their own demise? Realistically that's not likely to happen, which is where splash potions come in useful – they can be thrown at mobs or other players so that they're forced into contact with the effect. Cunning!

HOW TO BREW AND USE

1 You'll need to combine a regular potion with gunpowder on your brewing stand to give it explosive properties. You can also combine water bottles with gunpowder to create splash water bottles that put out fires.

2 Once brewed, throw a splash potion to use it. Splash potions don't last as long as regular potions. When throwing them at mobs or players, aim for their head to ensure they last for the maximum duration.

3 When a splash potion hits its target (a player or block), it will explode, releasing its contents. Any mobs or players within an 8.25 x 8.25 x 4.25-block area centered on the impact spot will be affected. The splash potion bottle will break when used and you won't be able to retrieve it.

WHEN TO USE

1 Unlike regular mobs, undead mobs (zombies, zombie pigmen, skeletons, wither skeletons, the wither, spider jockeys and chicken jockeys) are harmed by splash potion of healing.

2 Splash water bottles will deal 1 point of damage to endermen and blazes. They will also put out fires when thrown at a block, and their flame-quenching effects will extend to the 4 blocks surrounding the impact block.

3 You can cure a zombie villager of its zombification by throwing a splash potion of weakness at it, then feeding it a golden apple.

4 Splash potions can also be launched from dispensers so that you can release large volumes.

5 Undead mobs are healed by splash potion of harming, but all other mobs and enemy players will be harmed by it.

LINGERING POTIONS

True to its name, this variant of splash potion creates a cloud that lingers on the ground. Only the most advanced players will be able to brew lingering potions – the key ingredient is dragon's breath, which is incredibly difficult to get hold of.

HOW TO BREW AND USE

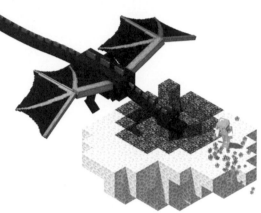

1 Collect dragon's breath by using a glass bottle when you're in or near to the ender dragon's breath attack. Be very careful – the dragon's breath will harm you.

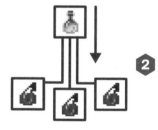

2 Brew 3 bottles of your chosen splash potion with the dragon's breath to create a lingering potion.

3 Throw your lingering potion and it will explode on impact with a solid block, creating a cloud of the potion's effect. On impact the cloud will extend to a radius of 3 blocks, eventually decreasing to 0 blocks over the course of 30 seconds. After 1 second, any player or mob that walks into the cloud will be imbued with the status effect of the potion. The amount of time the lingering potion effects will last for varies depending on the potion.

WHEN TO USE

 Undead mobs will be harmed by lingering potions of healing, and other hostile mobs are harmed by lingering potions of harming.

2 Lingering potions can also be launched out of dispensers, which can be incorporated into your base defences.

3 Lingering potions can be crafted with arrows to create tipped arrows. These handy projectiles will imbue their target with the corresponding status effect. The effect of a tipped arrow only lasts one eighth of the amount of time the potion itself lasts.

ARROW RECIPE

→ 4

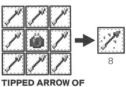

TIPPED ARROW OF SLOWNESS RECIPE

→ 8

NATURALLY OCCURRING BREWING EQUIPMENT

Having an "off day"? Not feeling up to a trip to the Nether? Happily, some of the items you need for brewing potions can be found naturally in the Overworld and they're yours for the taking if you know where they're hidden.

WITCHES AND WITCH HUTS

You'll find a cauldron filled with a random potion in each witch hut in swamp biomes. Witches may drop a potion of healing, fire resistance, swiftness or water breathing, if they're killed while drinking that potion. Witches spawn in any biome at light levels of 7 or lower, and in witch huts.

IGLOOS

Igloos can be found in ice plains and cold taiga biomes. Half of igloos contain a basement, and if you venture down to explore you'll find a brewing stand containing a splash potion of weakness.

END CITIES

2 potions of healing can be found in a brewing stand on the ships in End cities. These cities generate on the outer islands of the End dimension.

ADVANCED SORCERY

Congratulations – you're officially an advanced sorcerer. In this section you'll learn how to use enchantments and potions in clever combinations and discover how to build a suitably impressive sorcerer's house from which to practice your craft.

COMBOS

Whether you're mining deep underground or visiting the End, there's a combination of enchantments and potions that will give you the upper hand. These clever combos are perfect for advanced players.

MINING

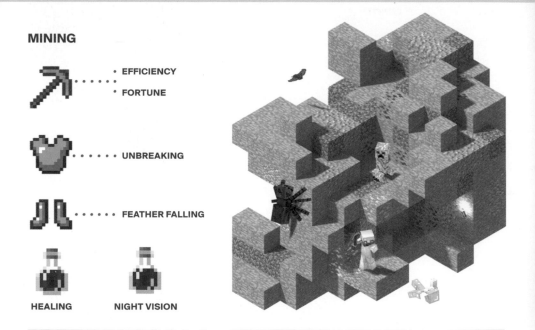

- EFFICIENCY
- FORTUNE

UNBREAKING

FEATHER FALLING

HEALING   NIGHT VISION

EXPLORING

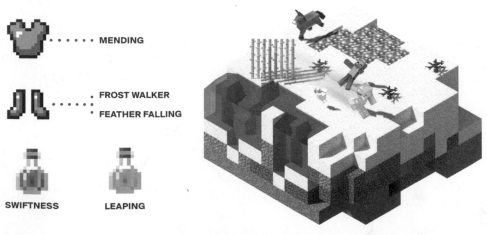

MENDING

- FROST WALKER
- FEATHER FALLING

SWIFTNESS   LEAPING

MOB COMBAT

. . . . . . FIRE ASPECT
. . . . . . BANE OF ARTHROPODS

. . . . . . FLAME
. . . . . . INFINITY

. . . . . . UNBREAKING

HARMING   STRENGTH

PVP COMBAT

. . . . . . SMITE

. . . . . . KNOCKBACK
. . . . . . POWER

. . . . . . PROTECTION

. . . . . . UNBREAKING

HEALING   STRENGTH

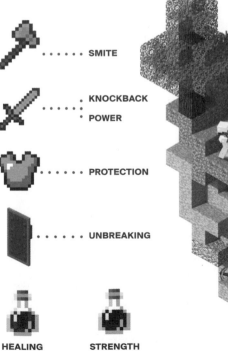

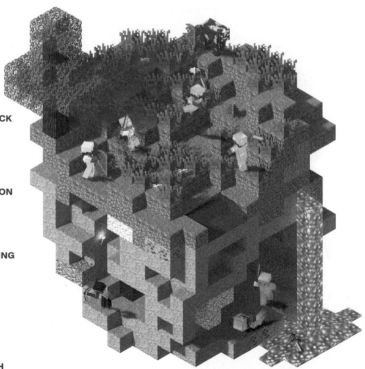

NIGHT

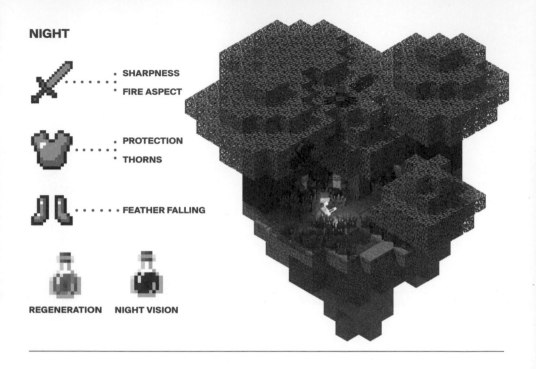

- SHARPNESS
- FIRE ASPECT

- PROTECTION
- THORNS

- FEATHER FALLING

REGENERATION   NIGHT VISION

UNDERWATER

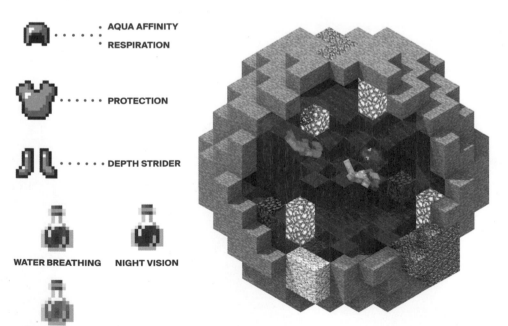

- AQUA AFFINITY
- RESPIRATION

- PROTECTION

- DEPTH STRIDER

WATER BREATHING   NIGHT VISION

REGENERATION

THE NETHER

 ········· • LOOTING
                     • SMITE

 ········· • MENDING
                     • FIRE PROTECTION

 ········· • PROJECTILE PROTECTION

FIRE RESISTANCE   INVISIBILITY

THE END

 ········· • INFINITY
                     • FLAME

 ·········· • PROJECTILE PROTECTION

 ·········· • FEATHER FALLING

STRENGTH   HEALING

WATER

SORCERER'S HOUSE

This sorcerer's house is largely built from stone and wood blocks, but it's the smaller details that make it truly magical. Various Nether materials and swamp-like elements are used to set the scene for sorcery.

YOU WILL NEED:

SCHEMATICS

These plans show the sorcerer's house from various perspectives so you can see how it's constructed. The brewing tower emerges from the roof of the main build and the inside layout has been carefully considered to maximize the available space.

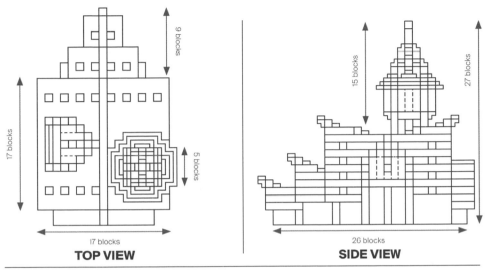

TOP VIEW

9 blocks

17 blocks

5 blocks

17 blocks

SIDE VIEW

15 blocks

27 blocks

26 blocks

GROUND FLOOR

25 blocks

15 blocks

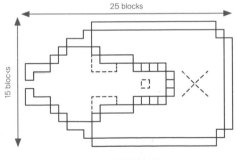

FIRST FLOOR

15 blocks

14 blocks

IDEAL LANDSCAPE

The witchy nature of the sorcerer's house makes it particularly suited to a gloomy swamp biome, which may already be inhabited by a witch. It would also sit nicely in a forest or roofed forest due to the shadows cast by the dense trees.

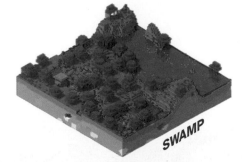

SWAMP

SORCERER'S HOUSE INTERIOR

 The open-plan ground floor is illuminated by glowstone blocks set into the floor, and this is where the enchanting area is set up. See pages 74-77 for a step-by-step guide to building the hidden library around the enchantment table.

 Take one of the staircases from the ground floor up to the first floor, which is carpeted in alternating blocks of purple and white. It's used for storage and houses a Nether portal, which allows you to easily visit the Nether to collect potion supplies.

3 You'll find the entrance to the brewing tower tucked away in the corner – a simple ladder leads up to the next floor.

4 The brewing area sits at the top of the tower – with 6 brewing stands at your disposal, you can quickly brew large quantities of potions.

5 The first floor of the brewing tower is ideal for storage. You can keep all your potion ingredients in four handily positioned chests.

THE HIDDEN LIBRARY

This hidden library build employs clever redstone mechanics to create an impressively mystical effect. Your bookshelves will rise up from the floor, as if by magic, when you approach your enchantment table.

 Build this shape – it's 5 blocks along the front with 2 blocks at the back. This is the first part of your base.

TIP

Make sure you have enough space in your sorcerer's house to build the hidden library – the base is approximately 8 x 9 blocks and 12 blocks high.

2 Extend the shape to form a rectangle (9 x 8 blocks). Don't forget to add the extra blocks in the center. This forms the complete base for your library.

3 Lay redstone dust as shown, with a repeater set to 1 tick (the default setting).

Now build a vertical transmission using 3 redstone torches and 3 additional blocks. This allows the redstone signal to travel upward.

Place 9 sticky pistons next to the central repeaters. The repeaters will power the sticky pistons. You will need to place blocks under the sticky pistons first, then destroy them.

Now add 9 more repeaters all set to 1 tick on top of the central blocks (facing inward).

7 Build this additional shape, attached to the top of the vertical transmission. It should follow the same pattern as the rear and sides of the base layer.

8 Lay redstone dust and a repeater across the top. Make sure you add the torch to the rear face of the block at the top front left corner to reverse the signal. Now add 9 more repeaters as shown.

9 Add 9 more sticky pistons, facing downward. The repeaters will power the sticky pistons.

12 That's it! Now you'll be magically greeted by a full complement of bookshelves each time you approach your enchantment table.

11 Place a bookshelf on the face of each sticky piston (that's 18 in total). The sticky pistons will move the bookshelves up and down when activated by a player standing on the pressure plate.

10 To build a platform for your enchantment table, place a solid block (we've used wood planks) directly above the central-most redstone dust and place a pressure plate on top. The enchantment table sits behind the pressure plate, on top of another solid block.

FINAL WORDS

Complicated stuff, right? But whoever said that using eldritch powers to rework the fabric of the universe would be easy? And, I hope you agree, as strange, cryptic and elaborate as these magical practices may be, the benefits are rather awesome. Whether you don glimmering gear that lets you shrug off the damage from explosive blasts, enchant your armor to prickle enemies who dare get too close, or slug back a brew to help you see through the dark, you'll find enchantments and potions give you the edge in many a perilous situation. Plus, "Sorcerer" looks pretty good on a business card, too. Bonus.

MARSH DAVIES
THE MOJANG TEAM

STAY IN THE KNOW!

GUIDE TO:
CREATIVE

GUIDE TO:
EXPLORATION

GUIDE TO:
THE NETHER & THE END

GUIDE TO:
REDSTONE

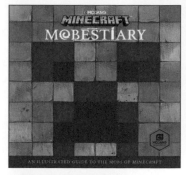

Learn about the latest Minecraft books
when you sign up for our newsletter at
RANDOMHOUSEBOOKS.COM/MINECRAFT

DEL REY

MOJANG